Diving Deep into Data Structures

From Simple Arrays to Advanced Trees

Table of Contents

Chapter 1. Introduction

In this essential Special Report, "Diving Deep into Data Structures: From Simple Arrays to Advanced Trees," we invite you to embark on a comprehensive exploration of the underlying mechanisms that fortify the world of programming. From the most basic arrays that form the bedrock of coding, to the labyrinthine complexity of advanced trees that organize and process data with astonishing efficiency, this report offers a careful examination of these critical components in a digestible and engaging fashion. Whether a seasoned technician aiming to broaden your knowledge base or a curious newcomer searching for a path into this technical realm, this report simplifies these concepts into understandable, compelling content. It is set to unravel the mystique around these fascinating architectural foundations in computer science, providing valuable insights that could serve as an essential tool in your developmental journey. Purchase your copy today, and dive deep into the matrix of data structures in a way you never thought possible.

Chapter 2. Unraveling the Basics: Arrays and Their Utility

Introduction to Arrays === An array is one of the most basic data structures in computer programming, and it forms the atomic building block for most software applications. Implemented as a sequential collection of similar data types, an array allows the storage of data points in a structured, organized manner. The ability to store multiple values in a single variable makes arrays an extremely efficient data structure in terms of memory usage and retrieval efficiency.

The primary virtue of arrays lies in their simplicity and their effectiveness to deal with binary memory systems modeled by modern computers. In its most primitive sense, an array can be viewed as an ordered collection of bytes slotted next to each other in memory, accessible through a numerical index that reflects the offset of a particular item from the start.

2.1. Characteristics of Arrays

Arrays have a number of defining characteristics that set them apart from other data structures. These characteristics include:

2.2. Array Operations

Homogeneity: All elements of an Array are of the same type, ensuring a uniform interpretation of the memory segment.

In order to use arrays effectively, it is important to understand the basic operations that can be performed on them. These operations constitute the primary interactions a developer undertakes with an array, and often determine its usability in a particular context.

Deletion: While not directly possible due to its static nature, deletion in an array usually involves overwriting or ignoring a certain value.

Understanding and Implementing Arrays in Different Programming Languages === While the basic principles of arrays remain consistent, their implementation varies slightly across different programming languages. The following sub-sections offer a brief overview of array usage in some of the popular programming languages.

2.3. Arrays in Python

In Python, arrays are defined using the list() function by default, though an explicit array module exists for more complex needs. Dynamically sized, with the provision to contain different data types, Python lists introduce a level of flexibility rarely seen in other languages.

2.4. Arrays in Java

In contrast, Java approaches the concept of arrays in a more traditional way. Defined with a fixed size at creation, Java arrays can hold one type of data, ensuring type safety but sacrificing some elements of flexibility.

2.5. Arrays in JavaScript

JavaScript, similarly to Python, uses a flexible array implementation. An array in JavaScript can change its size during runtime and can hold elements of different data types. This brings added flexibility but can cause type-related issues.

Use Cases and Applications of Arrays === Despite their simplicity, arrays fill a multitude of roles in the world of computer programming.

2.6. Data Handling

Due to their structured and organized nature, arrays are used for sorting and searching operations, implementing stacks and queues, and serving as a basis for other data structures like linked lists and trees.

2.7. Memory Management

Given an array's ability to store large amounts of data in contiguous memory locations, they are vital tools for efficient memory management in computing systems.

2.8. Buffering and Caching

Arrays often serve as buffers in I/O operations, or caches in memory to speed up access times for frequently fetched information.

In conclusion, arrays are deceptively simple but are a crucial part of nearly every software application. They underpin the functioning of more advanced data structures and algorithms and serve as a fundamental component of efficient data management and memory use. A firm grasp of the nature of arrays, their operations, and their applications, is, therefore, key for anyone eager to dive deep into the world of computer programming. With this knowledge, you are on your way to understanding more complex concepts that will enrich and optimize your programming experience.

Chapter 3. Variables and Constants: The Core Principles

Few elements are as foundational to programming as variables and constants. These two constructs serve as repositories for storing and manipulating information throughout a program's lifecycle. Valuable in virtually all coding applications, from simple tinkerings to complex algorithms implementation, variables and constants are the bread and butter of a developer's toolbox.

3.1. Variables: The Essence of Fluidity

Variables, as the name suggests, represent values that can vary throughout the lifespan of a program. In different programming languages, syntax and naming conventions for variables might differ, but the inherent concept remains consistent. Variables associate a name (identifier) with a memory location where the data is stored. This allows the user or the program itself to store, retrieve, or manipulate this data.

A basic operation to declare and assign a value to a variable would look like the following:

```
myVar = 5;
```

Here, myVar is the variable's name, and 5 is its assigned value. Note that the statement ends with a semicolon, which acts as a sentence's period in many programming languages.

We often say that a variable "holds" a value. However, a more accurate analogy might be that a variable is like a labeled box where we store our data.

3.2. Constant: The Pillars of Stability

Contrary to variables, constants remain immutable throughout the program, meaning that once a value is assigned to a constant, it cannot change. Because of this immutability, constants are often used to set values that aren't meant to alter. For example, the numerical value for Pi (3.14159...) or the number of days in a week (7).

Here's a crude syntax to declare a constant:

```
const PI = 3.14159;
```

In this scenario, PI stands as the constant's name housing the value 3.14159.

Programming languages differ in syntax when declaring constants. const, final, and define are all keywords used in different languages. Constants are typically named using all uppercase, with underscores between words. This scheme makes constants stand out, signaling that these shouldn't be modified.

3.3. Data Types: Categorizing Variables and Constants

Each variable or a constant that a programmer declares has a data type. The data type tells us the nature of data that can be stored, the amount of space allocated for that data, and the types of operations we can perform.

1. **Primitive Data Types:** They are the most basic form of data types, that include integer (`int`), floating-point (`float`), character (`char`), boolean (`bool`), and more. Their operational behavior varies, but these types represent the building blocks of data manipulation in most languages.

2. **Derived Data Types:** These types are transformations or compositions of primitive types and sometimes other derived types. They often include arrays, functions, and pointers.

3. **User Defined Data Types:** As the name suggests, these types are defined by the user and may include classes, interfaces, enumerations, and others.

Each of these different data types can be stored in a variable or constant, shaping the kind of operations that can be performed on it.

3.4. Variable Scope and Lifetime

The scope of a variable refers to the region within the code where the variable can be accessed. If declared outside of all functions, the variable is accessible from any point in the code, making it a global variable. If declared within a function, it's a local variable and can only be accessed within that function.

The lifetime of a variable is the period during the program's execution during which the variable exists in memory. For local variables, their lifetime is as long as the function is running. For global variables, their lifetime extends throughout the program execution.

3.5. Conclusion

Understanding how to effectively use and manipulate variables and constants is core to mastering any programming language. They provide the fundamental construct of data storage in code from which all other operations propagate. By mastering variables and constants, you can develop efficient and effective code, irrespective of the challenges thrown your way.

Chapter 4. Data Types: Exploring Strings, Booleans, and More

In our adventure into the realm of data structures, we begin at the roots - Data Types. They are the base data units upon which all structures and algorithms hinge, and their thorough understanding is the cornerstone for any budding programmer or seasoned code linguist.

4.1. A Look at Data Types

Data Types, in the simplest terms, are different types of data that a programming language can recognize and upon which it can perform operations. They are the building blocks of all programming and consist of simple types such as numbers and Booleans, as well as more complex types like strings and arrays.

4.2. The Numeric Data Type Club

Starting with the more straightforward of the data types, the Numeric type, in essence, encapsulates integers and floating-point (or decimal) numbers.

Integers are essential for counting and ordering things while float numbers, which come with a decimal point, can handle values with fractions. To consider a couple of examples in Python:

```
miles_travelled = 500  # Integer
average_speed = 75.5  # Float
```

The Integer and the Floating-Point Numbers are both considered as Numeric Data Types, even though they handle different types of numeric information. The language's ability to understand and work with these different numeric types is fundamental to all computing.

4.3. Journey into Strings

A step away from the simplicity of integer and decimal numbers, Strings make their entrance. Strings are made up of sequences of characters. This broad definition encompasses any data that can be represented as text, from actual words to gibberish sequences like 'jhdfhj749uhsdk'.

For instance, your name, "Hello, World!", and even the complete works of William Shakespeare can all be represented as Strings in a program.

```
greeting = "Hello, World!"  # String
```

Strings are very versatile. They can be concatenated (joined together), sliced (divided into smaller strings), and much more. However, unlike numbers, mathematical operations generally do not apply to strings.

4.4. The Binary World of Booleans

Moving on, we reach the unassuming yet extremely effective boolean data type. Named after mathematician George Boole, boolean data type is as straightforward as complicated gets - it can either be `True` or `False` (yes or no, 1 or 0, on or off). Booleans gain their true power in conditional statements, where they decide the path your program takes.

```python
is_raining = False  # Boolean
```

When you start dealing with logic and making your code make decisions, the Boolean value proves crucial.

4.5. More Data Types

While Numeric types, Strings, and Booleans cover a lot, they don't cover everything. There are other data types as well, such as the List data type in Python, which can contain a list of other data types, and the Tuple and Dictionary types, which are used to hold collections of data.

We will explore these more complex and exotic data types in upcoming chapters, taking our understanding of data types to a new level as we continue our journey through the vast world of data structures.

As we delve deeper, we'll explore the intrinsic connection between these data types and data structures, and how understanding this relationship can aid you in writing efficient and readable code.

4.6. Practical Essence of Each Data Type

Despite the range of their complexities, each data type has a significant role to play in different scenarios. For simple counts, integers work perfectly well. But when precision is key, the decimal-supporting float comes into play. Strings are the ubiquitous choice for handling text data, while Booleans shine when dealing with logic-based decision paths.

Understanding the fundamental characteristics of each of these data types is critical in laying a solid foundation in programming. Exploiting their distinct functionalities not only optimizes your code but also makes it robust and versatile.

4.7. Closing Notes on Data Types

In essence, Data Types are at the heart of programming. They channel the ability of a language to understand the data it is dealing with, and upon that knowledge build logical structures. Be it the process of storing, recalling, or manipulating data - everything begins with the humble data type.

Our exploration doesn't end here, but we've made an excellent start towards understanding the building blocks of the programming world. We'll continue delving deeper, unraveling the intricacies of more advanced data structures in the ensuing chapters.

Purchase your copy today for a full exploration of the content that awaits! From primitive data types to complex data structures, our resultant knowledge will be nothing short of profound. Let's keep digging, coding, learning, and evolving, in this incredible journey called programming.

Chapter 5. Linking it All Together: An Introduction to Linked Lists

If we imagine our data as nodes residing across a town, then the linked list would be the set of roads connecting each node. Rather than storing data contiguously like arrays, linked lists store data elements in separate nodes linked together, each holding its own data and the address of the next node. With their dynamic structure and efficient insertions and deletions, linked lists are an instrumental part of data structures toolbox. Let's take a more in-depth look.

5.1. What is a Linked List?

A linked list is a linear data structure similar to an array. However, unlike arrays, elements are not stored in a particular memory location or index. Rather, each element is a separate object that contains a pointer or a link to the next object in the list. Each element (commonly called nodes) consists of two items: the data and the reference to the next node. The last node has a reference to null. The entry point into a linked list is called the head of the list. It is a reference to the first node in the linked list. The list of nodes present in the linked list is traversed starting from the head and ending at the last node which points to null.

```
struct Node {
    int data;
    Node* next;
};
```

```
Node* head;
```

The elements are not stored at contiguous memory locations which allow structures to be resized at run-time.

5.2. Types of Linked Lists

There are several types of linked lists:

1. **Singly Linked List**: This type of list has a pointer which points to the next node in the sequence. In the case of a single list, traversing is unidirectional, from the head to null.

2. **Doubly Linked List**: As the name suggests, this type of list has two references associated with each node, one to the next node and one to the previous node. This characteristic allows us to traverse in both directions: forward and backward.

3. **Circular Linked List**: In a circular linked list, the system forms a circle. In other words, the link field of the last node points to the first node.

These types offer flexibility and powerful capabilities to your programs, depending on the requirements of your application.

5.3. Operations on a Linked List

A number of operations can be performed on linked lists including:

- Insertion: We can insert an element at the beginning, at the end or after a given node in the list.

- Deletion: An element can be deleted using the key. The element can be anywhere in the list.

- Display: We can display the complete list.

- Search: We can search for an element in the list.

```cpp
void insertNode(Node** head, int newValue) {
    Node* newNode = new Node();
    newNode->data = newValue;
    newNode->next = (*head);
    (*head) = newNode;
}

void deleteNode(Node **head, int key) {
    Node* temp = *head, *prev;

    if (temp != NULL && temp->data == key) {
        *head = temp->next;
        delete temp;
        return;
    }

    while (temp != NULL && temp->data != key) {
        prev = temp;
        temp = temp->next;
    }

    if (temp == NULL) return;

    prev->next = temp->next;

    delete temp;
}

void printList(Node *node) {
    while (node != NULL) {
        cout<<" "<<node->data;
        node = node->next;
    }
}
```

5.4. Time Complexity of Operations

While performing operations on a linked list, the time complexity matters. The search operation in a linked list has time complexity O(n). However, the delete and insert operations have time complexity O(1), if we have a pointer to the node where the operation needs to be performed.

5.5. Conclusion

With the ability to insert and remove nodes, linked lists offer a flexible and efficient data structure with many uses. The lack of need to define an initial size makes them practical for situations where it is not clear how many nodes will be in the list. Linked lists are a foundational data structure, and understanding these lists is a step towards a stronger data structure and algorithm foundation.

Chapter 6. Making Your Life Easier: What are Stacks and Queues?

Stacks and queues are two forms of data structures that are fundamental to the world of programming. They are dynamic in nature, allowing values to be stored and removed, with distinct principles dictating how this process operates. They also have numerous applications, from managing memory allocation and execution calls, to determining the chronology of functions in a program.

6.1. An Overview of Stacks

A stack is a linear data structure that strictly adheres to a principle known as Last-In-First-Out (LIFO). This principle means that the last item inserted or pushed into the stack is the first one to be released or popped out. This is likened to a real-world stack, such as a pile of plates; you normally add (push) or remove (pop) plates from the top.

To better grasp this concept, it is essential to understand the primary operations of a stack:

- **Push:** It involves adding an element to the collection. In the context of stacks, new elements are always added on top.

- **Pop:** It involves removing an element from the collection. In accordance with the LIFO principle, elements at the top (most recently added ones) are the ones removed.

- **Peek (or Top):** This operation allows you to view what's on top of the stack, without modifying it.

6.2. Implementing Stacks

Now let's delve into how you can construct a stack. You can use an array or a linked list. In the following example, we will use an array for simplicity. Visualize the array as a column that receives elements from the top.

Here is a simple Python code snippet that creates a Stack class:

```python
class Stack:
    def __init__(self):
        self.stack = []

    def push(self, item):
        self.stack.append(item)

    def pop(self):
        if len(self.stack) < 1:
            return None
        return self.stack.pop()

    def peek(self):
        return self.stack[-1]

    def size(self):
        return len(self.stack)
```

We defined an array (`self.stack`) to hold the elements of the stack. For the `push` and `pop` functions, we've utilized Python's built-in `append` and `pop` methods, which inherently follow the LIFO principle. The `peek` function allows us to inspect the top element, while `size` gives the current number of items in the stack.

6.3. Applications of Stacks

The LIFO principle of stacks makes them ideal for a variety of use-cases in programming:

- **Managing Function Calls:** Programming languages utilize stacks to manage function calls. This mechanism, known as the call stack, tracks active subroutines or functions.

- **Memory Allocation:** Stack-based memory allocation stores local variables and function parameters, released when their scope is exited.

6.4. Understanding Queues

A queue, like a stack, is a linear data structure. However, it works on the principle of First-In-First-Out (FIFO). This means that the first element added (enqueue) to the queue will be the first one to be removed (dequeue).

An excellent analogy to understand queues is a real-world queue, like at a supermarket checkout. The person who gets in line first will be the first one to be served and leave the queue.

Key operations associated with queues include:

- **Enqueue:** Add an element to the end of the queue.

- **Dequeue:** Remove an element from the front of the queue.

- **Peek (or Front):** Get the value of the front of the queue without removing it.

6.5. Implementing Queues

You can implement a queue using different data structures, like arrays or linked lists. For simplicity, let's use an array for this implementation. Visualize the array as a horizontal row that receives elements from the right side (rear) and releases them from the left side (front).

Here is a Python code snippet that creates a Queue class:

```python
class Queue:
    def __init__(self):
        self.queue = []

    def enqueue(self, item):
        self.queue.append(item)

    def dequeue(self):
        if len(self.queue) < 1:
            return None
        return self.queue.pop(0)

    def peek(self):
        return self.queue[0]

    def size(self):
        return len(self.queue)
```

In this case, `self.queue` is an array that holds the elements. The `enqueue` function adds elements to the rear of the queue, and `dequeue` removes them from the front. To inspect the front element, you use the `peek` function. The `size` function returns the current number of items in the queue.

6.6. Applications of Queues

The FIFO nature of queues enables their use in scenarios where order and fairness are required, for example:

- **Serving Requests:** In computer science, queues keep track of requests, ensuring they are processed in the order of their arrival.

- **Handling Buffers:** Printers or live video streaming applications often use queues as buffers to handle data before it's sent to the device.

Understanding and utilizing stacks and queues are not just key for any coder seeking to deepen their understanding of data structures, but they are also fundamental to unlocking a greater understanding of how computation operates on a granular level.

Chapter 7. Organizing Data: The Power of Hash Tables

A hash table, sometimes also referred to as a hash map, is a data structure that offers fast operations in storing and retrieving data. They map keys to values, operating as an efficient indexer that directly navigates us to the memory location of the value we're looking to find. By providing a way to maintain data that can be quickly searched, hash tables are extremely vital in various applications ranging from database indexing to caches.

Let's dive into understanding these powerful machines in greater detail.

7.1. Understanding Hash Tables: An Overview

The magic behind the efficiency of hash tables stems from the hash function. The hash function operates on the keys and produces an output that reveals the address inside the table where the corresponding value is stored. Keys are unique identifiers attached to elements, and the hash function transforms the key into the index, ensuring that every unique key maps to a unique index.

Hash functions need to maintain consistency-- every time a key is put into the function, it needs to always return the same result. If it didn't, hash tables wouldn't maintain their efficiency. Locating the value would become a significant challenge.

7.2. Collision in Hash Tables: What happens when two keys hash to the same index

Hash collisions happen when two different keys hash to the same index. This becomes problematic as it defeats the purpose of having unique indexes for every unique key. There are various strategies to handle collisions, two of them being chaining and open addressing.

Chaining: When a collision happens, the hash table stores multiple items that hash to the same index in the form of a linked list. This approach ensures that every hashed index holds a unique linked list.

Open Addressing: In this strategy, whenever a collision occurs, it looks for the next available slot. There are different ways to measure the next open slot, such as linear probing, quadratic probing, or double hashing.

7.3. Hash Table Operations

Hash tables significantly improve the speed of principal operations such as searching, inserting, and deleting. With an ideally distributed hash function, these operations are often a constant time, O(1), complexity.

The effectiveness of hash tables comes with a caveat, though. They depend highly on the efficiency of the hash function. When badly distributed, the hash function can cause a lot of collisions leading to decreased performance.

7.4. Applications of Hash Tables

Hash tables, given their ability to store and retrieve data so effectively, have a wide range of applications in computer science:

Database Indexing: Hash tables are widely used in database indexing where each value is assigned a unique key. Associative arrays in database operations use hash tables.

Caches: Many cache implementations use hash tables for storing data. Web page caches, disk sector caches, and memory caches use hash tables extensively.

Compiler Operations: Compilers use hash tables for symbol table construction, where variable names are keys and their properties are values.

Networking: Switches in network routers use hash tables to route incoming requests to the correct outgoing port.

7.5. Conclusion

Hash tables, though simple in their operation, are a powerful construct in computer science. Understandably, the largesse of their role might seem overwhelming. However, by appreciating their systemic efficiency and understanding the mechanisms surrounding collisions and hash functions, one can truly leverage the ubiquitous power of hash tables. It's a representation of an elegant principle in computer science - sometimes, the most potent systems depict the most simple, subtle design.

Chapter 8. Building on Foundations: An Insight into Graphs and Their Applications

Data structures are paramount to efficient data handling and manipulation in computer science. Among them, the graph data structure stands prominently due to its wide applicability and versatility in problem-solving. It is ubiquitous, finding use in networking, social media management, mapping, search engines, and numerous other use-cases. In this chapter, we shall dive deep into graphs, understanding their fundamental makeup, types, representations, traversals, and ultimately, their importance in various applications.

8.1. Understanding Graphs

At their core, graphs are a robust form of a data structure consisting of vertices (nodes) and edges (links) connecting these vertices. In terms of Abstract Data Types (ADT), graphs are viewed as sets complemented by a binary relation. The first set represents vertices, while the second constitutes the edges. This binary relationship can be thought of as a connection, whereby a pair of vertices is associated with an edge. It is crucial to note that this definition is for an undirected graph, one where edges are bidirectional. Directed graphs, on the other hand, have edges with directions, similar to one-way streets.

8.2. Types of Graphs

Graphs come in various shapes and sizes, but they primarily fall into two categories: directed and undirected graphs. Undirected graphs have edges that do not have a specific direction. That is, if there is an edge between node A and node B, you can traverse from A to B and vice versa. Conversely, directed graphs, also known as digraphs, have edges with distinct directions. In this case, if there is a directed edge from node A to B, one can only travel in that specific direction, from A to B, but not the reverse.

Another way to categorize graphs is by their edge characteristics. There are three major types: simple, multigraph, and pseudo graph. A simple graph has only one undirected (or directed in the case of digraphs) edge between any two nodes with no loops. Multigraphs allow parallel edges between the same vertices, and pseudo graphs permit self-loops with a node linking to itself.

8.3. Representing Graphs

Two predominant methods exist for representing graphs in the memory: adjacency list and adjacency matrix representation.

Adjacency List Representation: Here, an array of lists is used, where the size of the array equals the number of vertices in the graph. Each node in this array corresponds to a graph vertex. The list at each array index holds all the vertices adjacent to the vertex related to that index.

Adjacency Matrix Representation: This method uses a two-dimensional matrix for its representation. The size of this matrix is VxV, where V is the number of vertices in the graph. If there is an edge between vertices I and J, the entries [i][j] and [j][i] (for undirected graph), or just the entry [i][j] (for directed graph) in the matrix are set to 1, otherwise, they are set to 0.

8.4. Graph Traversals

Graph traversal is the process of visiting each vertex in a graph. This efficient scanning of all vertices and edges is crucial for many applications. Two well-known techniques for graph traversal are the Depth-First Search (DFS) and Breadth-First Search (BFS).

DFS utilizes a stack data structure with a LIFO (Last In First Out) mechanism. It visits a node and explores as far as possible along each branch before backtracking.

BFS uses a queue data structure with a FIFO (First In First Out) mechanism. It visits all adjacent nodes of the start node before moving onto the nodes at the next level.

8.5. Graph Applications

The application of graphs spans various domains. Here are some notable ones:

1. **Pathfinding**: Graphs are used in GPS and mapping services for shortest path finding algorithms like Dijkstra's and A*.

2. **Computational Biology**: Studies of genetic structures, protein networks, or organism interdependencies can be effectively modeled using graphs.

3. **Social Networks**: Graphs serve as the backbone to model and analyze social interactions.

4. **Web Crawlers**: Search Engines use graph theory to index and rank web pages based on networks of links.

To wrap it up, graphs offer robust and flexible structures to encapsulate complex relationships between data points, making them crucial players in practical problem-solving. Understanding the nuances of graph theory will undoubtedly arm you with a powerful tool in your computational arsenal.

Chapter 9. Playing with Nodes: Understanding Trees and Binary Trees

Welcome to the world of trees and binary trees—a mesmerizing little universe of nodes and connections as complex and beautiful as a fractal pattern.

9.1. Defining the Tree

The word 'Tree' paints a warm, familiar picture in our minds—a sturdy trunk with an intricate network of branches sprouting out, sporting leaves. The computer science conception of 'Tree' isn't drastically different; it too is a well-structured, hierarchical arrangement brimming with nodes instead of leaves, with each node holding a piece of data.

Let's break it down: A tree in our context is a collection of entities called 'nodes' interconnected by 'edges.' Each tree has a top node, known as the 'root.' Every node—apart from the root—has a clear, direct path going back to the root. Any two nodes are connected by exactly one edge. Nodes with no children are known as 'leaf nodes,' embracing their botanical counterpart.

Let's visualize things in a simplified asciidoc visual:

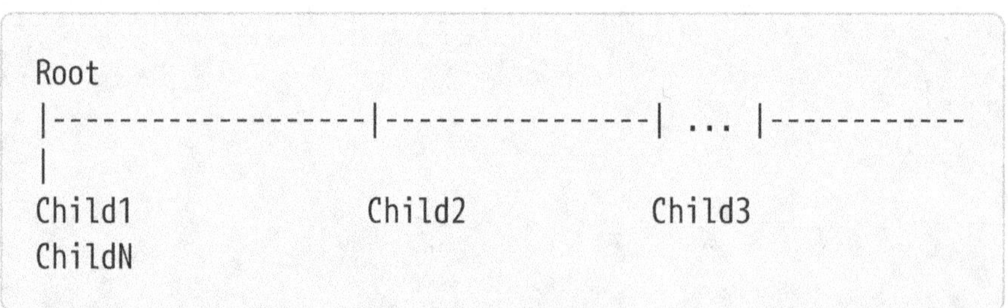

Each child, in turn, can be a root of its own sub-tree, leading to an endless potential for nested structures.

9.2. Understanding Binary Trees

The transition from a generic tree to a 'Binary Tree' is an easy one. As the term implies, binary trees are those where each node can have a maximum of two children, typically referred to as the 'left child' and the 'right child.'

Here's how it looks in asciidoc visual representation:

```
          Node
        /      \
  Left child  Right child
```

Binary trees are incredibly useful and are at the heart of some of the most powerful data structures and algorithms in computer science, including Binary Search Trees, AVL Trees, Red-Black trees, Heaps, and Syntax trees.

9.3. Relationship Between Nodes

Nodes in a tree share a unique relationship, similar to the one we share with our ancestors and descendants. In a tree, if there is a link from node 'A' to node 'B', then 'A' is parent to 'B', and 'B' is a child of 'A'.

Using asciidoc syntax, a basic parent-child relationship would appear as:

In a binary tree, node 'A' could have up to two children 'B' and 'C', structured like so:

```
        A
       / \
      B   C
```

Nodes sharing a parent are referred to as 'siblings.'

9.4. Important Properties of Trees and Binary Trees

The "path" in a tree is a sequence of nodes connected by edges. The "length" of this path is defined as the number of transitions between the nodes. The "depth" of a node is the length of the path from that node to the root. The "height" of a node is the length of the longest path from that node to a leaf. The height of the tree is the height of the root node.

The maximum number of nodes at level 'l' of a binary tree is 2^l. For a binary tree with 'n' nodes, the minimum possible height is $\log(n+1)$, making binary trees desirable for their compact, efficient packaging of data.

9.5. Traversing a Tree

One of the crucial aspects of handling trees and binary trees is the traversal—the process of visiting (checking and/or updating) each node in a tree data structure, exactly once. The way you traverse a tree can have immense implications on the speed and efficiency of your program. Let's delve into three primary ways of doing this: Pre-

Order, In-Order, and Post-Order traversals.

- **Pre-Order Traversal**: In this type of traversal, the process is to visit the root node first, then the left subtree, and finally the right subtree.

- **In-Order Traversal**: Here, we first visit the left subtree, then the root node, and finally the right subtree.

- **Post-Order Traversal**: In this method, we first visit the left subtree, then the right subtree, and finally the root node.

9.6. Implementing Trees and Binary Trees

Implementing trees and binary trees involves creating a data structure for the node which comprises the data element and pointers to its children. In the case of a binary tree, you would need one for the left child, and another for the right child.

In upcoming sections, we'll work on examples using multiple programming languages, and compare their efficiencies in terms of time and space complexity. Understanding how to work with trees and binary trees will thereby equip you with tools to deal with more complex, intricate structures and algorithms, thereby amplifying your programming skillset.

Remember, trees are not just a data structure; they are a critical foundation of computing—used in databases, file systems, and even in the language syntax. By mastering trees, you can ensure you are providing the most efficient, reliable solutions in your programming endeavors.

This chapter is the starting point of your journey with trees and binary trees. Practice diligently, and always keep exploring. As the saying goes, the sky's the limit, except in the world of programming—

with trees, there's simply no limit at all.

Chapter 10. Advanced Structures: Navigating Binary Search Trees

Just as a hospital uses a hierarchical system - doctors, nurses, paramedics - to meet the demands of its patients, a binary search tree (BST) applies a similar ranking strategy to organize data. Through its unique structural framework, the BST can streamline searches, insertions, and deletions in an efficient manner. It is time for us to chart the unexplored terrains of this ingenious mechanism of the programming realm.

10.1. Introduction to Binary Search Trees

Binary search trees (BST) are node-based data structures that feature striking characteristics: each node has a unique key and two distinguished subtrees, often referred to as the left and right subtrees. The key rule of BST is that for any given node, all keys in its left subtree are less than the node's key, while all keys in the right subtree are greater. This property is recursively true for all nodes and provides the basis for efficient search operations.

Consider a typical binary search tree arranged as follows:

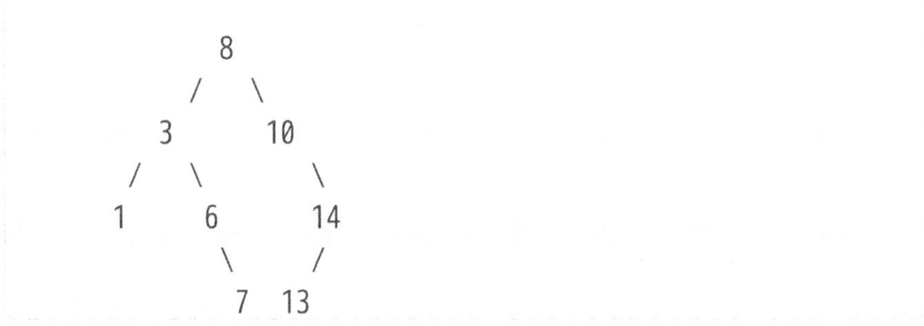

In this binary search tree, the root node is 8. All nodes in the left subtree (3, 1, 6, and 7) are less than 8, and all nodes in the right subtree (10, 14, and 13) are more than 8. This method of organization creates an efficient path towards any particular node during search operations.

=== Searching in a Binary Search Tree

The searching algorithm traverses down the tree from the root to either the left or right subtrees depending on the key's value, much like the decision-making process in the "Guess a Number" game. It provides a time complexity that is hard to beat - O(h), where h is the height of the tree.

Here's a basic algorithm you can use to search an element in BST:

if root is NULL then return NULL; if root.key is equal to the search key then return root; else if root.key is greater than the search key then return search(root.left, key); else return search(root.right, key);

=== Insertion in a Binary Search Tree

Similar to searching, the operation of insertion starts at the root node and navigates down to the correct position to place the new node. Time complexity here is also O(h).

A simple process for insertion could look something like this:

if root is NULL then create a node with key as root; if root.key is bigger than the key then root.left = insertNode(root.left, key); else if root.key is less than the key then root.right = insertNode(root.right, key); return root;

Deletion in a Binary Search Tree

Data removal opens up an empty spot in the BST, and to maintain the binary search tree property, this position must be filled appropriately. Deletion could involve three distinct scenarios; when the target node has no child, one child, or two children.

With no child, the process is straightforward - we merely remove the node. If the node has one child, we replace the node with its child. But for nodes with two children, we locate the in-order predecessor or the in-order successor and replace the node with it (either will work). After this, we delete the in-order successor or predecessor, which will now be a case of either having one child or no child, hence completing the recursive operation.

Insertion and deletion operations ensure the BST keeps its property even when its structure changes, allowing for efficient subsequent operations.

Tree Balancing

Sometimes, BSTs can become skewed if the inserted keys are already sorted. In these cases, the search time becomes linear - $O(n)$, where n is the number of nodes. To keep the efficiency of BSTs, various balancing algorithms like AVL, Red-Black, and B-trees are applied. These carefully rotate and reposition nodes to maintain the BST property and ensure faster access times.

Binary search trees form an essential core of how data is parsed and interpreted, providing quick search options and adaptable data configurations. Their dynamics make them an invaluable tool for any programmer's toolkit.

Remember, a solid understanding of data structures, their limitations, and potentials is key to becoming an efficient and effective programmer. So leverage the power of binary search trees, and let your code traverse the heights of programming efficiency.

Cutting-Edge Concepts: Digging into AVL and B-trees

In the world of data structures, two key concepts that revolutionize data organization and efficiency are AVL trees and B-trees. The intrinsic balancing mechanisms of these advanced tree structures significantly improve search efficiency.

Introduction to AVL Trees

The first thing one needs to understand about AVL trees is the balance factor. An AVL, named after its inventors Adel'son-Vel'skii and Landis, is a self-balancing binary search tree. For each node in such a tree, the height of the left and right subtrees differs by at most one.

The height of a node in a tree is the number of edges on the longest path from the node to a leaf. The balance factor of a node is the difference between the height of its left child and its right child. Therefore, an AVL tree is one where every node has a balance factor of -1, 0, or 1.

AVL Tree Operations

There are three standard operations that an AVL tree can perform: insertion, deletion, and searching.

- *Insertion:* When inserting a node, first it follows the standard binary search tree insertion process, then it gets to the task of ensuring that the tree remains balanced. If the balance factor of any node is not -1, 0, or 1 after the insertion, a rotation operation will be performed to restore the balance.

- *Deletion:* Deletion in an AVL tree also follows the standard binary search tree deletion process. However, after the deletion operation, the tree might need re-balancing. The rebalancing process is similar to the one performed during insertion.

- *Searching:* Searching in an AVL tree is faster compared to a normal binary search tree due to its balancing property, which maintains the height of the tree to a logarithm of the number of nodes.

=== Rotations in AVL Trees

The key to maintaining balance in an AVL tree lies in rotation operations - single and double rotations - aimed at correcting any imbalance in the tree.

Single Rotations:

- *Right-Right Case (RR):* A single left rotation is needed for this case.

- *Left-Left Case (LL):* A single right rotation is needed for this case.

Double Rotations:

- *Left-Right Case (LR):* First a left rotation, followed by a right rotation is needed for this case.

- *Right-Left Case (RL):* First a right rotation, followed by a left rotation is needed for this case.

Rotations help restabilize the tree after insertion or deletion operations. They rotate unbalanced nodes in specific ways to ensure that no node in the tree has a balance factor less than -1 or greater than 1.

=== Introduction to B-Trees

The B-Tree is a self-balancing search tree, conceived by Rudolf Bayer and Edward M. McCreight with the objective of maximizing data access efficiency by keeping the data sorted and allowing for efficient insertion, deletion, and search operations.

The B-tree is an extension of the binary search tree, allowing for more than two child nodes. This adaptability enables B-trees to manage the complexities of disk and large system navigation, where read times are costly, and thus reducing the number of disk reads is crucial for efficient operation.

=== B-Tree Properties

Some critical properties fundamentally define the B-tree structure:

- *One Root:* A B-tree contains one root, which may be the only node in the entire tree.

- *Degree:* The minimum number of children a non-leaf
and non-root node can have is defined by the degree of
the B-tree (denoted by 't').

- *Keys:* Each node can contain at most 2t - 1 keys. The
keys of a node act as separation values which divide its
subtrees. They help to decide which subtree to traverse
during search operation.

- *Children:* Each node can have at most 2t children.

- *Root Node:* The root node must have at least two
children if it is not a leaf node.

- *All Leaf Nodes at Same Level:* All leaf nodes must be
at the same level, ensuring that access time to retrieve
any individual record is always the same, optimizing the
search operation.

=== B-Tree Operations

There are typically three standard operations that a B-
tree can handle: searching, insertion, and deletion.

- *Searching:* Search operation in a B-Tree starts from
the root and moves towards the leaf nodes comparing
search element with keys in nodes.

- *Insertion:* The insertion operation needs to ensure
that the B-tree properties remain intact after the
insertion. If a node is full (i.e., has 2t -1 keys), a
split operation is performed during the insertion
process.

- *Deletion:* Deletion in a B-tree is more complex.

After the deletion of a key, if the number of keys is less than the minimum required, keys are either moved from a neighboring node or the node is merged with a neighbor.

From intricate balancing properties to rotation and split operations, AVL trees and B-trees represent some of the most complex but efficient data structures used in modern programming. They form the backbone of various databases and file systems, enabling efficient and faster data access. Understanding these tree structures could be the key to digging deeper into the intricate world of data structures and algorithms.

Remember, the stronger the base, the better the understanding of the complex. Deep diving into AVL and B-trees is that strong base you need for your data structures journey. As you traverse these nodes, remember each balancing act, each rotation, and split operation, is a lesson taking you closer to mastering these fundamental yet complex data structures.